Greenhaven World History Program

GENERAL EDITORS

Malcolm Yapp
Margaret Killingray
Edmund O'Connor

Cover design by Gary Rees

ISBN 0-89908-211-4 Paper Edition
ISBN 0-89908-236-X Library Edition

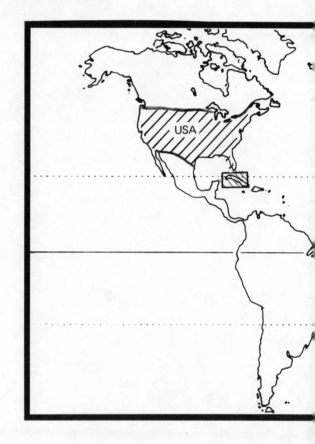

First published in Great Britain 1975 by
GEORGE G. HARRAP & CO. LTD
© George G. Harrap & Co. Ltd. 1975

THE COLD WAR

by Alasdair Nicolson

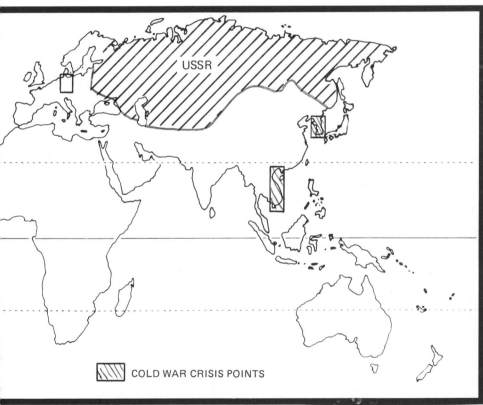

USSR

COLD WAR CRISIS POINTS

Greenhaven Press, Inc.
577 SHOREVIEW PARK ROAD
ST. PAUL, MN 55112

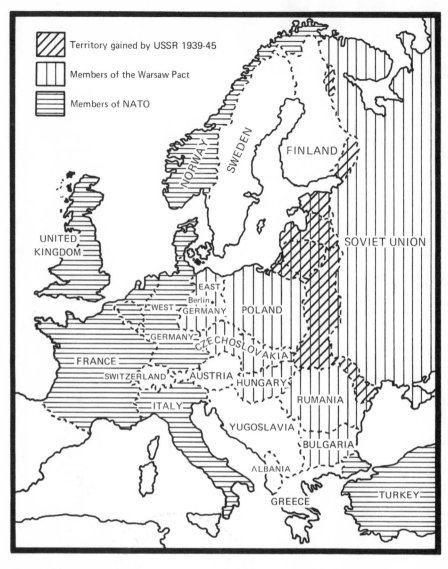

Legend:
- ▨ Territory gained by USSR 1939-45
- ▥ Members of the Warsaw Pact
- ▤ Members of NATO

Countries labeled on map: NORWAY, SWEDEN, FINLAND, UNITED KINGDOM, SOVIET UNION, EAST GERMANY, Berlin, WEST GERMANY, GERMANY, POLAND, CZECHOSLOVAKIA, FRANCE, SWITZERLAND, AUSTRIA, HUNGARY, RUMANIA, ITALY, YUGOSLAVIA, BULGARIA, ALBANIA, GREECE, TURKEY

The Cold War in Europe

Everyone knows what a war is. It is when people fight each other. But what is the Cold War? It is the name which has been given to a long period, lasting from 1946 until the 1960s and beyond, when the two most powerful states in the world quarrelled but did not actually fight each other. In this booklet we shall be looking at three questions — why they quarrelled; why they did not actually go to war with each other; and what effect their quarrel had on the rest of the world.

The two great states were the USSR (Union of Soviet Socialist Republics) and the USA, (United States of America), or as most people say, Russia and America.

Each had their allies. The Russians were supported by the countries of eastern Europe and America by the countries of western Europe. So the two alliances were often called the East and the West. Most of the rest of the world tried to keep out of the struggle but it was not possible for any country to escape completely from its effects.

The Cold War had many causes but if one had to pick just one it would be fear. Russia feared America and America feared Russia. America and Russia had very different ways of running their countries. Each feared that the other wished to destroy their way of life. Each side had different views about how the world was going to develop in the future. The Russian leaders were communists, that is they believed that, after a struggle between classes, a new world would come into being in which all men would be equal, all property belong to everyone and there would be no state power. In the meantime, ever since the Russian revolution of 1917 they had built up a system in which the state had tight control over the way most things were run. They expected that revolution and the communist system would spread throughout the world and

Members of Western Alliances
NATO, SEATO, CENTO.

The Western alliances and the Soviet Union

3

Greek government commandos on patrol during the Greek civil war 1946-49. The Greek communists made several attempts to seize control of the country, but Stalin failed to give them any real support

they encouraged communists and revolutions in other countries.

The American leaders did not like communism. In the first place they thought that it did not work and that people were much better off under their system of capitalism or free enterprise. Secondly they thought that communism meant loss of freedom; the communist countries seemed to them like great prison camps, ruled by the police. They also said that talk of revolution was just an excuse for Russia to take over other countries. They actively tried to prevent communism spreading in other states. Both Russia and America were 'super-powers' with enormous armed forces and therefore each feared attack from the other.

EUROPE IN 1945

During the Second World War Russia and America had fought together to defeat Germany in Europe. *(The Two World Wars)** But before the war had ended the Russians and Americans were already suspicious of each other. Russia wanted to protect herself against the chance that she would be attacked again, in the way Germany had attacked her in 1941. She had already occupied large parts of eastern Europe before the war, moving her frontier further west. As the Russian army pushed back the Germans during the war and liberated the countries of eastern Europe, she set up friendly (socialist) governments. The frontier

4 *Titles in brackets refer to other booklets in the Program
**The reference (D) indicates the numbered documents at the end of this book

between these countries and western Europe came to be called the 'iron curtain'. (D1)** The Russians also wanted to protect their long southern border by making agreements with all the countries from Turkey to Korea, so as to make sure that the USSR was strong and no enemy could threaten her from that direction.

To the Russians this seemed just good sense, but to the West it looked quite different. As they saw it, Russia was threatening to control a large part of Asia and Europe and, in particular, had forced the people of eastern Europe to accept governments that they did not want. Western European countries were afraid of this Russian advance. They looked to America for help and protection. The American armies, therefore, remained in western Europe. The United States was the natural leader of the Western Alliance. She was the richest power in the world. She could provide the men and weapons to help defend Europe. And she alone had the most powerful weapon ever known − the atom bomb. No matter how many more soldiers the Russians had, would they dare to attack if America could bomb all their cities to the ground? President Truman of the USA declared that communism was 'an evil force' which suppressed individual liberty and he pledged the USA to support 'free peoples' everywhere. (D2)

At the end of the war Europe faced serious social and economic problems. Industry, farms and railways had been destroyed and

Ruins of the German Reichstag, or Parliament, in Berlin at the end of the Second World War. In 1945 Germany was defeated, divided up and occupied by the wartime allies, Russia, the United States, France and Britain

US President Harry Truman. In laying before Congress his Truman Doctrine he said, 'I believe that it must be the policy of the United States to support free peoples who are resisting attempted subjugation by armed minorities or by outside pressures'

millions of people were homeless refugees. George Marshall, American Secretary of State, introduced the Marshall Plan by which all countries could share in the US aid – as long as they agreed on a planned programme for European recovery. (D3) The offer was a generous one and Britain, France and most western nations quickly accepted it. The Russians, however, regarded it as an attempt by the Americans to control Europe, and refused to allow any communist country to share in the American offer.

GERMANY

The main quarrel between Russia and America, however, was over Germany. Germany was seen by Russia as the major threat to world peace. Indeed, Nazi Germany led by Hitler had caused the war, and ruined Europe. Scarred on Russian minds was the memory of the twenty million Russians who had died during that war. Germany (and Berlin, the German capital) was now divided up into four occupation zones (British, American, French and Russian) and thus seemed weak and divided but Russian suspicions still persisted.

The fact that Russia and America were now quarrelling created difficulties for the four power systems of government in Berlin. Berlin lay deep inside the Russian zone of Germany and it was quite isolated from the rest of western Germany run by the western allies. The western allies wished to have control in their own zone of Berlin, but Russia wanted the whole of Berlin to become part of her zone of Germany.

THE BERLIN BLOCKADE

In June 1948, on the excuse of stamping out currency rackets, the Soviet Union blockaded all land routes to the city. The western allies broke the blockade by ferrying in supplies by air. The use of military power to break the blockade would probably have led to another major war in Europe. But the West felt that if they did not tackle this Russian threat promptly the future safety of other western nations would be threatened. Already that year a communist government supported by Russia had gained control of Czechoslovakia.

For about eleven months West

Berliners watching a US aircraft ferrying food and supplies during the Western airlift to break the Russian blockade of Berlin in 1948

Berlin depended completely on the use of the narrow air corridors into the city. Only the barest essentials were allowed in on the incoming planes. The diet of the West Berliner was meagre indeed — dehydrated (dried) vegetables, dried milk, tinned meats, very little sugar and butter. Fuel for heating was very strictly rationed and the electricity supply was severely cut. (D4) The air lift however, succeeded and when the Soviet Union lifted the blockade in May 1949 over 2,000,000 tonnes of supplies had been flown

The Cold War in East Asia

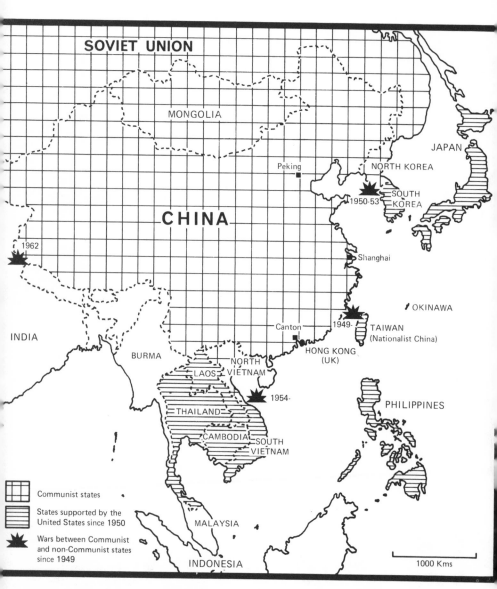

SOVIET UNION

MONGOLIA

Peking

NORTH KOREA

JAPAN

1950-53 · SOUTH KOREA

CHINA

1962

Shanghai

OKINAWA

Canton · 1949· TAIWAN (Nationalist China)

INDIA

BURMA

HONG KONG (UK)

NORTH VIETNAM

LAOS

1954·

PHILIPPINES

THAILAND

CAMBODIA SOUTH VIETNAM

Communist states

States supported by the United States since 1950

Wars between Communist and non-Communist states since 1949

MALAYSIA

INDONESIA

1000 Kms

8

in and over 300,000 flights had been made by the air forces of the western allies.

THE NATO ALLIANCE

The West had won one important round in the Cold War, and no battles had been fought. The western allies now drew closer together under the American 'shield'. The Americans joined in a new alliance of western nations called the North Atlantic Treaty Organization. (D5) The NATO alliance had its military head-quarters in France.

THE KOREAN WAR

The Americans regarded the Pacific area as being within their sphere of influence. They had occupied the defeated Japan by themselves in 1945. In 1949 when China, under Mao Tse-Tung, became a major communist state, the Americans feared a spread of communism in Asia. Russia, the ally of China, was also a Pacific power. She wanted to see China recognized as a Pacific power and to gain a larger place for herself in the area. But the United States refused to recognize the new communist China and continued to support the defeated Nationalists who had retreated to the island of Taiwan (Formosa).

The quarrel between East and West in Asia came to a head over Korea. At the end of the war, in 1945, Korea, part of the Japanese empire, had been divided; the north was supervised by the Soviet Union and the south by the Americans. In June 1950, after several years of bickering between the two now independent parts of the country, the communist north

United States infantry advancing through a ruined village during the Korean War. US troops formed the bulk of the United Nations forces fighting the North Koreans and the Chinese. American casualties were very high in the war

invaded the south and almost overran the whole country. The USA fearing that the communists might gain control of the whole country appealed to the United Nations for help. Soon a fifteen nation force was engaged in battle against the North Koreans. This was the first war between East and West. However, Russia and America were not directly fighting each other, although American troops formed the largest part of the United Nations force.

The tide of battle soon turned against North Korea and UN troops swept north towards the Chinese-Korean border. China had not been officially involved in the war but, fearing for her own safety, she sent a 'volunteer' army of 150,000 men to fight alongside the North Koreans. The Chinese attack was so powerful that the American commander of the UN force feared a complete defeat and threatened to bomb Chinese supply bases in Manchuria. The results of such action might have led to a general war, involving Russia and atomic weapons. But the commander was sacked and by 1951 peace talks got under way.

As a direct result of the Cold War in Asia the Americans were able to gather round them a group of friendly nations who were pledged to defend the area from the spread of communism. Their alliance was called the South East Asia Treaty Organization. (SEATO) The Americans also

A woman looks at the ruins of her home in Pyongyang, the capital of North Korea, after a United Nations air raid on the city. Large areas of Korea were devastated in the war of 1950-53

John Foster Dulles, the US Secretary of State for Foreign Affairs in the 1950's

built up further alliances with countries in the Middle East. The main aims were to prevent the spread of communism southwards from the Soviet Union by building a ring of military bases round her southern frontiers, and to safeguard the supplies of oil, essential to the western countries. (D6)

THE NUCLEAR BALANCE

By 1953 the Russians had drawn equal with the Americans not only in terms of atomic knowledge but also in terms of the production of the latest atomic weapons. The use of one of these bombs by either side might have finished the Korean war but would have led to immense

Nikita Krushchev, the Russian premier, addressing the United Nations General Assembly in 1960

destruction. A new kind of relationship between the two super-powers was required which would rule out the use of nuclear weapons. Russia and America re-examined their policies towards each other, realizing that they would have to live together in peace.

The Russian dictator Stalin died in 1953. His successor, Krushchev, introduced a new 'co-existence' policy. He wanted to trade with the West. He was confident that peaceful competition would soon show which was the better of the two systems: the western democratic system or the Soviet socialist system. Both sides now appeared to show a more human face to each other. The West too appeared to be responding to the more friendly approach of the Russians.

President Eisenhower of the USA proposed an 'Open-Skies' scheme of aerial surveys to open up information about the whereabouts of military bases on both sides of the 'iron curtain', in order to reduce the possibility of war, (D7) but the Russians did not accept the proposal.

THE COLD WAR 1955–62

Unfortunately the optimism of both sides was dampened by several setbacks. The first setback was the establishment of the Warsaw Pact which was the Russian answer to the NATO alliance. The Soviet Union had now gathered round her all the communist nations of eastern Europe. It was natural that the Russians would build up such an alliance but it led to many tense moments when the armies of each side moved close to each other along the 'iron curtain'. This tension grew even more when West Germany was re-armed by the western powers and became a member of NATO.

Then there were anti-Russian revolts in Hungary and Poland in 1956. When it appeared that the Hungarian revolt had succeeded, Krushchev ordered his army to restore order in Hungary. The West felt that if Russia could crush this tiny nation with such force there seemed little hope for 'peace and tolerance' between East and West. (D8)

Another cause of suspicion came in 1960 when high flying American spy planes flew over Soviet territory. The Americans denied that such flights took

The Berlin Wall, built by the East German authorities in 1961, finally sealed East Germany off from the West

place, but the Russians shot down one plane and imprisoned the pilot for spying on Russia.

THE BERLIN WALL

In 1949 the occupation of Germany ended, but troops from both sides still remained in Germany. The French, British and American occupation zones eventually became the Federal Republic of Germany, or West Germany; while the Russian zone became the German Democratic Republic, or communist East Germany. Berlin was also divided in half, but it lay right in the middle of East Germany. The border between East and West Germany was heavily guarded but people could move freely between the east and west zones of Berlin. During the 1950s thousands of East Germans fled to the more prosperous West Berlin and thence to West Germany. Many of these people were skilled and professional workers and East German industry began to feel their loss. Therefore, in 1961 the East Germans built a high wall across Berlin which was heavily guarded. (D9) Some East Germans who tried to escape over the wall were shot. Many people in the West felt that this proved

Fidel Castro giving one of his long speeches just after he had gained control of Cuba in 1959. On Castro's right is Che Guevara, one of his lieutenants in the Cuban revolution who was later killed in South America trying to start another war

how bad the communist system was.

THE CUBAN CRISIS

In 1959 guerilla armies led by a young revolutionary named Fidel Castro, overthrew the brutal dictator, Batista, on the Caribbean island of Cuba. Castro disliked American military and economic power which dominated the states of Central and South America and which he believed

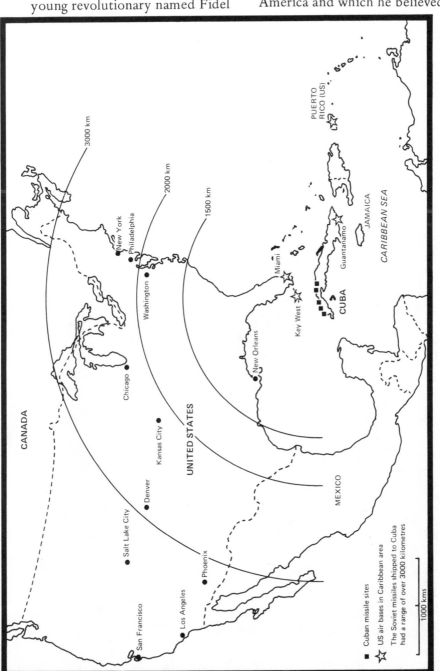

The Cuban missile threat 1962

- ■ Cuban missile sites
- ☆ US air bases in Caribbean area

The Soviet missiles shipped to Cuba had a range of over 3000 kilometres

1000 kms

had kept Batista in power for so long. Castro was a communist and the new socialist government which he set up, had increasingly strong links with Russia. For the first time Russia had an ally in Latin America and on an island only a hundred miles from the United States.

The Americans had an important military base in Cuba and they wanted to make sure that it was safe. They therefore supported an attempt by exiled Cubans to invade the island and oust Castro from power. This was a complete failure but it convinced Castro that he should seek support from the Soviet Union in case the Americans tried to invade again. The Cubans asked the USSR for military aid and heavy Soviet rockets and other weapons began to arrive in Cuba in 1962. The Americans were very worried. If these Soviet weapons were established in Cuba there was a real threat that the NATO defence system would be broken — not from *outside* but from *within* the American area. Military experts examined carefully the possibilities for the future. If nuclear rockets were set up in Cuban territory they could be used to destroy vast areas of America.

President Kennedy decided to declare 'a quarantine on all offensive equipment to Cuba'. The US navy and air force prepared to prevent any Soviet freighters

Photograph taken by a US reconnaissance aircraft showing missiles aboard a Russian ship bound for Cuba in 1962

suspected of carrying missiles, from reaching Cuba. Naturally, if these ships were stopped or interfered with by the Americans it was expected that the Soviet Union would take some serious action — possibly bombing the USA. A nuclear war loomed as a real danger.

On 24th October there were eighteen Soviet ships heading for Cuba and towards the American patrols. At dawn on 24th October all the Soviet ships turned round and headed for home. Mr. Krushchev had backed down. The world was saved from war.

The two sides now entered into negotiations about how to end the crisis and in the end a compromise was reached. (D10,11,12) Russia agreed to withdraw all missiles and dismantle the bases. The USA promised to lift the naval blockade and not to invade Cuba.

The effects of the Cuban crisis were most important. The super-powers — Russia and America — agreed that such a bitter quarrel must not happen again. It had been too dangerous. Indeed, because of the seriousness of the crisis both agreed to look at ways of developing 'peaceful co-existence'. To help closer contact a special telephone link between Washington and Moscow was set up.

VIETNAM

After Korea, the other country which was a source of dispute

United States aircraft spraying the forests of South Vietnam with defoliants in an attempt to destroy cover used by communist guerillas

between China and the Americans was Vietnam. This Southeast Asian country was also divided between communist north and non-communist south and a long bloody war developed during the 1960s with more and more American troops becoming involved (D13) Much of the fighting was guerilla war in the jungles and villages of South Vietnam. Support for the guerillas came from communist North Vietnam. The Americans helped the South Vietnam government to fight the guerillas in the south while her aircraft bombed the supply lines from the north. The war dragged on for many years but it never spread beyond Indo-China nor did China and Russia become directly involved. (D14) America bombed but did not invade North Vietnam, stopping short of any action which might lead to a major war involving China and Russia.

Despite American use of all kinds of conventional (non-nuclear) weapons in the war, she was unable to defeat the guerillas or stop North Vietnamese aid. The American troops were finally withdrawn from South Vietnam after a cease-fire agreement in 1972, although fighting in Indo-China still continued.

PEACEFUL COEXISTENCE

After the Cuban crisis there were occasions when the western powers found themselves confronting the Soviet Union. But despite these periods of tension and the long war in Vietnam, the bitterness was very much reduced after 1963. There were several reasons for this.

The national leaders were now more acutely aware of the effects of nuclear war. They had been testing nuclear weapons for some years and they now feared the further spread of nuclear weapons to other nations, and the increasing radioactivity in the world. Within a few months of the Cuban crisis Britain, the USA and the USSR agreed to ban the testing of nuclear devices in the air, outer space and under water — a first step towards nuclear control. *(The Atom Bomb)*

By the mid 1960s neither Russia nor America was the undisputed leader of the East and West blocs. Russia could no longer count on the absolute loyalty of her communist allies. Yugoslavia had been the first to show her independence of Russia as early as 1948. The Rumanians later pursued a policy of brisk trade and lively tourist traffic with the West despite Russian opposition. Albania also turned away from Russia. In Czechoslovakia new leaders relaxed controls and allowed greater freedoms. Russia feared that Czechoslovakia might leave the Warsaw Pact. In 1968 along with her other allies in eastern Europe she invaded Czecho-slovakia and overthrew the more liberal government. But the tendency towards a freer life and greater prosperity for the peoples in the communist countries of east Europe continued. Thus by the early 1970s the Soviet Union was seeking trade agreements and closer contacts with many western countries, including West Germany, the cause of many of her fears in the earlier stages of the Cold War.

Russian tank faced by an angry crowd of Czechs during the Soviet occupation of Prague in 1968

China had become a much more important country in international affairs since 1963. China and Russia had themselves quarrelled about Russian help to China and about the long border between the two countries. They also argued about how to bring about communism. As a result China had become less dependent on Russia and led a rival group of communist countries who often disagreed with Russian policies. China adopted a new attitude of friendliness towards western countries and with her entry to the United Nations in 1972 improved contacts not only with countries in Asia and Africa, but even with the USA.

During the years after the second world war, many nations in Asia and Africa, which had been part of the colonial empires of Britain, France, Holland, etc. became independent. Their leaders, men like Nehru of India and Nkrumah of Ghana did not want their countries to become part of the West or East in the Cold War. They wished rather, to remain neutral and uncommited, forming a 'third world'. (D15)

As they became independent, these new nations joined the United Nations Organization and by the late 1960s they formed a large voting group which did not necessarily support either Russia or America. When the Organization was founded in 1945 it was dominated by the USSR and the USA and their followers. By 1970 there were nearly 150 members of the UN, including all the new nations of Asia and Africa. When communist China joined in 1972 and France began to take an independent anti-American line, the old division between East and West was no longer so clearcut.

Many Europeans too felt that Europe should act as a third world power between the USA and the Soviet Union, particularly with the European Economic Community (The Common Market) uniting many European countries. In the early 1960s France decided to withdraw from NATO and to act independently rather than follow the lead of the United States.

THE COLD WAR IN WORLD HISTORY

The Cold War was a time of great bitterness, tension and waste. In Korea and Vietnam there was the death and destruction caused by real war. In Germany and in other parts of the world families and peoples were divided from each other. Even within the super-powers there were groups who did not agree with their governments' policies and suffered for this. Was the Cold War all waste, then? We saw how, in 1945, the two super-powers were deeply divided by fear. Their fears were real and could not disappear over night. Both had to realise that they could not know what the future would be; that it would develop in ways they could not imagine. When they understood this and understood also that their societies were not quite as different from each other as they had thought, they were less eager to force their ways on each other.

At the same time the two super-powers had to come to grips with the fact that a war using the weapons they had created would destroy not only the enemy but also themselves and the rest of civilization as well. To avoid out-right war and to give time for greater understanding to develop was the achievement of the Cold War. Unpleasant as it was, it was much better than a hot one.

DOCUMENT 1

THE IRON CURTAIN   *WINSTON CHURCHILL — The British
Prime Minister during the Second World War, in a speech made on 5th
March 1946*

A shadow has fallen upon the scenes so lately lighted by the Allied
victory. Nobody knows what Soviet Russia and its Communist international organization intends to do in the immediate future, or what are
the limits, if any, to their expansive and proselytizing tendencies. I have
a strong admiration and regard for the valiant Russian people and for my
war-time comrade, Marshal Stalin. . . . We understand the Russians need
to be secure on her western frontiers from all renewal of German
aggression. We welcome her to her rightful place among the leading
nations of the world. Above all we welcome constant, frequent and
growing contacts between the Russian people and our own people on
both sides of the Atlantic. . . .

From Stettin in the Baltic to Trieste in the Adriatic, an iron curtain
has descended across the Continent. Behind that line lie all the capitals
of the ancient states of central and eastern Europe. Warsaw, Berlin,
Prague, Vienna, Budapest, Belgrade, Bucharest, and Sofia, all these
famous cities and the populations around them lie in the Soviet sphere
and all are subject in one form or another, not only to Soviet influence
but to a very high and increasing measure of control from Moscow. . . .

DOCUMENT 2

THE TRUMAN DOCTRINE   *HARRY TRUMAN — The American
president announcing, in a message to Congress on March 12 1947
that the USA would help countries which were threatened by
communism*

The peoples of a number of countries of the world have recently had
totalitarian regimes forced upon them against their will. The Government
of the United States has made frequent protests against coercion and
intimidation, in violation of the Yalta Agreement, in Poland, Rumania
and Bulgaria. I must also state that in a number of other countries there
have been similar developments.

At the present moment in world history nearly every nation must
choose between alternative ways of life. The choice is too often not a
free one.

One way of life is based upon the will of the majority, and is distinguished by free institutions, representative government, free elections, guarantees of individual liberty, freedom of speech and religion, and freedom from political oppression.

The second way of life is based upon the will of the minority forcibly imposed upon the majority. It relies upon terror and oppression, a controlled press and radio, fixed elections, and the suppression of personal freedoms.

I believe that it must be the policy of the United States to support free peoples who are resisting attempted subjugation by armed minorities or by outside pressures.

I believe that we must assist free peoples to work out their own destinies in their own way.

I believe that our help should be primarily through economic and financial aid which is essential to economic stability and orderly political processes.

DOCUMENT 3

THE MARSHALL PLAN   *GEORGE C. MARSHALL – The American Secretary of State in a speech made on 5th June 1947*

In considering the requirements for the rehabilitation of Europe the physical loss of life, the visible destruction of cities, factories, mines, and railroads was correctly estimated, but it has become obvious during recent months that this visible destruction was probably less serious than the dislocation of the entire fabric of European economy. . . . The town and city industries are not producing adequate goods to exchange with the food-producing farmer. Raw materials and fuel are in short supply. Machinery is lacking or worn out.

The truth of the matter is that Europe's requirements for the next 3 or 4 years of foreign food and other essential products – principally from America – are so much greater than her present ability to pay that she must have substantial additional help, or face economic, social and political deterioration of a very grave character.

It is already evident that, before the United States Government can proceed much further in its efforts to help start the European world on its way to recovery, there must be some agreement among the countries of Europe as to the requirements of the situation. It would be neither fitting nor efficacious for this Government to undertake to draw up unilaterally a program designed to place Europe on its feet economically. This is the business of Europeans. The role of this country should consist of friendly aid in the drafting of a European program and of later support of such a program so far as it may be practical for us to do so. The program should be a joint one, agreed to by a number, if not all European nations.

DOCUMENT 4

THE BERLIN BLOCKADE   *From the* Daily Express, *9th July 1948*

Two million people settled down in gloom tonight to obey new and drastic siege orders. There will be only 4 hours electric light a day, half in the morning, half in the evening.

All routine transport will stop from 6.00 p.m. to 6.00 a.m. The Western Powers have also cut off the power from Berlin's district railway. But the Russians say that they will supply the current.

Power for industry will be reduced by 80%. Only factories essential for the day to day life of the city will be supplied. Tonight 50% of Berlin's industrial workers face immediate unemployment. They will get a dole worth 60% of their normal wages.

Generator sets are being flown into Berlin by R.A.F. Yorks. They will provide light during the cuts for hospitals and other essential buildings.

The Britons in Berlin will have electricity for 8½ hours daily. Their clubs must serve cold meals only and shut at 10.00 p.m. Their bars will be shut from 8.00 p.m. to 9.00 p.m.

Riding has been banned to save fodder for horses which are now to have strict ration.

Wives and children in the French colony of 8000 have been advised to leave Berlin as soon as possible owing to the food shortage. They are already moving out (by air) at the rate of 250 a day.

DOCUMENT 5

THE NORTH ATLANTIC TREATY   *Extracts from the Treaty which was signed on 4th April 1949, by Belgium, Canada, Denmark, France, Iceland, Italy, Luxembourg, Netherlands, Norway, Portugal, the United Kingdom and the United States of America*

The Parties to this Treaty reaffirm their faith in the purposes and principles of the Charter of the United Nations and their desire to live in peace with all peoples and all governments.

They are determined to safeguard the freedom, common heritage and civilization of their peoples, founded on the principles of democracy, individual liberty and the rule of law.

They seek to promote stability and well-being in the North Atlantic area.

They are resolved to unite their efforts for collective defense and for the preservation of peace and security.

They therefore agree to this North Atlantic Treaty.

Art. 5. The Parties agree that an armed attack against one or more of them in Europe or North America shall be considered an attack against them all; and consequently they agree that, if such an armed attack occurs, each of them . . . will assist the Party or Parties so attacked by taking forthwith, individually and in concert with the other Parties, such action as it deems necessary, including the use of armed force, to restore and maintain the security of the North Atlantic area.

Any such armed attack and all measures taken as a result thereof shall immediately be reported to the Security Council. Such measures shall be terminated when the Security Council has taken the measures necessary to restore and maintain international peace and security.

DOCUMENT 6

A RUSSIAN VIEW   *A Russian student talks to a western visitor*
in 1958

Don't be a child who can't understand anything. The matter is very simple and any Soviet citizen can explain it to you. Imperialism is preparing to attack the USSR. The United States is surrounding us with bases which are ready to fire atomic bombs. Western Germany will soon possess the most powerful army in Western Europe, equipped with the new weapons of destruction. What does this mean? Does it mean peace? No, my dear, that's not true. In reality war is already going on. It is a war of nerves, an armament race, a hit-and-run battle. For this war to develop into open conflict is merely a question of time. It is a question of the ability of American imperialism to hold out, and this is already ending; pushed towards war by economic laws. Our society is constantly informed of this, and the more we stress our desire for peace, the more we strengthen the desire of the USA for aggression against the USSR and the countries of the People's Democracies.

DOCUMENT 7

THE OPEN SKIES PROPOSAL   *EISENHOWER — President of the*
United States presenting a statement on disarmament at the Geneva
Conference, 21st July 1955

I should address myself for a moment principally to the delegates from the Soviet Union, because our two great countries admittedly possess new and terrible weapons in quantities which do give rise in other parts of the world, or reciprocally, to the fears and dangers of surprise attack.

I propose, therefore, that we take a practical step, that we begin an arrangement, very quickly, as between ourselves — immediately. These steps would include:

To give to each other a complete blueprint of our military establishments, from beginning to end, from one end of our countries to the other; lay out the establishments and provide the blueprints to each other.

Next, to provide within our countries facilities for aerial photography to the other country — we to provide you the facilities within our country, ample facilities for aerial reconnaissance, where you can make all the pictures you choose and take them to your own country to study, you to provide exactly the same facilities for us and we to make these examinations, and by this step to convince the world that we are providing as between ourselves against the possibility of great surprise attack, thus lessening danger and relaxing tension. Likewise we will make more easily attainable a comprehensive and effective system of inspection and disarmament, because what I propose, I assure you, would be but a beginning.

DOCUMENT 8

LIBERATION   *JOHN FOSTER DULLES — US Secretary of State in 1953 giving his view of American policy towards communist countries and their peoples*

We shall never have a secure peace or a happy world so long as Soviet communism dominates one-third of all of the peoples that there are, and is in the process of trying at least to extend its rule to many others.

These people who are enslaved are people who deserve to be free, and who, from our own selfish standpoint, ought to be free because if they are the servile instruments of aggressive despotism, they will eventually be welded into a force which will be highly dangerous to ourselves and to all the free world.

Therefore, we must always have in mind the liberation of these captive peoples. Now, liberation does not mean a war of liberation. Liberation can be accomplished by processes short of war.

I ask you to recall the fact that Soviet communism, itself, has spread from controlling 200 million people some 7 years ago to controlling 800 million people today, and it has done that by methods of political warfare, psychological warfare and propaganda, and it has not actually used the Red Army as an open aggressive force in accomplishing that.

Surely what they can accomplish, we can accomplish. Surely if they can use moral and psychological force, we can use it; and, to take a negative defeatist attitude is not an approach which is conducive to our own welfare, or in conformity with our own historical ideas.

DOCUMENT 9

THE WARSAW PACT AND BERLIN   *This statement issued on*
13th August 1961, gives the East European view of the need for the
Berlin Wall

The western powers, far from having made any efforts to normalize the
situation in West Berlin, on the contrary continue to use it intensively as
a centre of subversive activities against the German Democratic Republic
and all other countries of the socialist commonwealth. In no other part
of the world are so many espionage and subversion centres of foreign
states to be found as in West Berlin and nowhere else can they act with
such impunity. These numerous subversion centres are smuggling their
agents into the German Democratic Republic for all kinds of subversion,
recruiting spies and inciting hostile elements to organize sabotage and
provoke disturbances in the German Democratic Republic. . . . The
governments of the Warsaw Treaty member states address the
People's Chamber and the government of the German Democratic
Republic and all working people of the G.D.R. with a proposal that a
procedure be established on the borders of West Berlin which will
securely block the way to the subversive activity against the countries of
the socialist camp, so that reliable safeguards and effective control may
be established round the whole territory of West Berlin, including its
border with democratic Berlin.

DOCUMENT 10

CUBA – 1   *KRUSHCHEV – In a letter about the Cuban missiles to*
President Kennedy, 6th October 1962

I have learned with great pleasure of your reply to Mr Thant to the effect
that steps will be taken to exclude contact between our ships and thus
avoid irremediable fateful consequences. . . . The main thing that must
be done is to normalise and stabilise the state of peace among states,
among peoples.
    I understand your concern for the security of the United States, Mr
President, because this is the first duty of a President. But we are worried
about the same questions: and I bear the same obligations, as Chairman
of the Council of Ministers of the USSR.
    You have been worried concerning the fact that we have helped Cuba
with weapons, with the aim to strengthen its defensive capacity – yes,
precisely, its 'defensive capacity', because no matter what weapons it
possesses, Cuba cannot equal you: because these are different quantities,
all the more so if one takes into consideration the modern means of
extermination.

Our aim has been, and still is, to help Cuba. And no one can deny the humaneness of our motives, which are to enable Cuba to live in peace and to develop in the way its people desires.

You want to make your country safe. This is understandable, but Cuba too wants the same thing. All countries want to make themselves safe.

But how are we, the Soviet Union, our Government, to assess your actions which are expressed in the fact that you have surrounded the Soviet Union with military bases; surrounded our allies with military bases; have disposed military bases literally around our country; have stationed your rocket armament there? This is no secret. American officials are demonstratively saying this.

Your rockets are situated in Britain, situated in Italy, and are aimed against us. Your rockets are situated in Turkey. You are worried by Cuba. You say that it worries you because it is a distance of 90 miles by sea from the coast of America, but Turkey is next to us. Our sentries walk up and down and look at each other. Do you consider then that you have the right to demand security for your own country and the removal of those weapons which you call offensive and do not acknowledge the same right for us?

You have placed destructive rocket weapons, which you call offensive, in Turkey, literally at our elbows. How then does the admission of our equal military capacities tally with such unequal relations between our great states? This cannot be made to tally in any way.

I think it would be possible to end the conflict quickly and to normalise the situation, and then people would breathe more easily, considering that the responsible statesmen have good sense and an awareness of their responsibility, and have the ability to solve complex questions and not bring things to a catastrophe of war.

I therefore make this proposal: We agree to remove from Cuba those means which you regard as offensive means; we agree to carry this out and make a pledge in the United Nations. Your representatives will make a declaration to the effect that the United States, on its part, considering the uneasiness and anxiety of the Soviet State, will remove its similar means from Turkey.

DOCUMENT 11

CUBA — 2   *PRESIDENT KENNEDY — In a White House statement, 27th October 1962*

Several inconsistent and conflicting proposals have been made by the USSR within the last twenty-four hours, including the one just made public in Moscow. The proposal broadcast this morning involves the security of nations outside the Western Hemisphere [i.e., Turkey]. But it is the Western Hemisphere countries and they alone that are subject to the threat that has produced the current crisis – the action of the Soviet Government in secretly introducing offensive weapons into Cuba. Work on these offensive weapons is still proceeding at a rapid pace. The first imperative must be to deal with this immediate threat, under which no sensible negotiations can proceed. . . . As to proposals concerning the security of nations outside this hemisphere, the United States and its allies have long taken the lead in seeking properly inspected arms limitation, on both sides. These efforts can continue as soon as the present Soviet-created threat is ended.

DOCUMENT 12

CUBA – 3   *PRESIDENT KENNEDY – In a letter to Krushchev on 27th October 1962*

I have read your letter of 26 October with great care, and welcomed the statement of your desire to seek a prompt solution to the problem. The first thing that needs to be done, however, is for work to cease on offensive missile bases in Cuba and for all weapons systems in Cuba capable of offensive use to be rendered inoperable, under effective UN arrangements.

Assuming this is done promptly I have given my representatives in New York instructions that will permit them to work out this week-end . . . an arrangement for a permanent solution to the Cuban problem along the lines suggested in your letter of 26 October.

As I read your letter, the key elements of your proposals – which seem generally acceptable as I understand them – are as follows:

(1) You would agree to remove these weapons systems from Cuba under appropriate UN observation and supervision; and undertake, with suitable safeguards, to halt the further introduction of such weapons systems into Cuba.

(2) We, on our part, would agree – upon the establishment of adequate arrangements through the UN to ensure the carrying out and continuation of these commitments – (a) to remove promptly the quarantine measures now in effect; and (b) to give assurances against an invasion of Cuba. I am confident that other nations of the Western hemisphere would be prepared to do likewise.

DOCUMENT 13

AMERICA AND VIETNAM   *DEAN RUSK – The American Secretary of State, in a speech on 18th February 1966*

We have sent American forces to fight in the jungles of that beleagured country because South Vietnam has, under the language of the SEATO Treaty, been the victim of 'aggression by means of armed attack'.

There can be no serious question as to the existence and nature of this aggression . . . by the Hanoi régime against the people of South Vietnam.

Beginning over a year ago, the Communists apparently exhausted their reservoir of Southerners who had gone North. Since then the greater number of men infiltrated into the South have been native-born North Vietnamese. Most recently, Hanoi has begun to infiltrate elements of the North Vietnamese Army in increasingly larger numbers. Today, there is evidence that nine regiments of regular North Vietnamese forces are fighting in organized units in the South.

I have reviewed these facts – which are familiar enough to most of you – because, it seems to me, they demonstrate beyond question that the war in Vietnam is as much an act of outside aggression as though the Hanoi régime had sent an army across the 17th Parallel rather than infiltrating armed forces by stealth.

DOCUMENT 14

CHINA AND VIETNAM   *In a letter to Ho Chi Minh, President of North Vietnam, on 30th January 1966, the Chairman of the People's Republic of China affirms Chinese support for North Vietnam, but does not mention direct military intervention by China*

I have received your letter of 24th January in which you strongly condemn the barbarous war of aggression waged by U.S. imperialism in Vietnam. . . . The Chinese Government and people firmly support the just stand of the Democratic Republic of Vietnam set forth in your letter.

U.S. imperialist aggression is the root cause of the present grave situation in Vietnam. It is clear to all that, according to the 1954 Geneva agreements, the Vietnam question should have already been settled. But the United States has thoroughly trampled underfoot the Geneva agree-ments under which it has assumed obligations. It has fostered its puppet regimes in southern Vietnam, obstructed the peaceful reunification of Vietnam, slaughtered or imprisoned hundreds of thousands of Viet-namese patriots and launched an inhuman 'special war' against the south Vietnamese people. As it failed to win the 'special war' it has sent over huge forces for direct aggression in southern Vietnam and employed its air force units to bomb the Democratic Republic of Vietnam. Obviously, the aim of the United States is to turn southern Vietnam into its colony and military base and perpetuate the partition of Vietnam. . . . The Chinese people always unswervingly stand together with the Vietnamese people and whole-heartedly support and assist them in their just struggle. To whatever extent may be the price we have to pay, we 650 million Chinese people will stand by the fraternal Vietnamese people in a joint struggle to thoroughly defeat the U.S. aggressors.

DOCUMENT 15

NATIONAL INDEPENDENCE   *PRIME MINISTER OF BURMA –*
Explaining in a speech to an American audience in 1955, why Burma, which was once a British colony, wished to be neutral

Burma has a long history. . . . The civilization, passed on to us by our forebears, has now become our national heritage. It is our way of life. We prefer it to any other way of life on this earth. We do not say that it cannot be improved, or that it cannot be adapted to suit modern conditions, but we do not wish to change its basis. We are not prepared to exchange it for any other way of life. . . . We therefore cannot be induced to give it up in exchange for some other way of life, be that the Communist way, the Western European way, the American way, or any other way. . . . We have concluded that in the present phase of our history, and the present state of the world, the wisest and even the only course for Burma is to pursue an independent policy, unshackled by . . . 'entangling foreign alliances'. . . . In the present circumstances of Burma, her membership in any alliance with a great-power military *bloc* is incompatable with her continued existence as an independent state. This may seem to be putting it strongly, but it is a fact. Our recent history is such, our experience with great powers is such, that in the minds of the people of Burma an alliance with a big power immediately means domination by that power. It means the loss of independence.

ACKNOWLEDGMENTS

Illustrations

The Imperial War Museum page 5; Keystone Press Agency pages
7, 9, 10, 12, 13, 14, 16, 17, 19; Radio Times Hulton Picture
Library pages 4, 6, 11.

Documents

D4, *Daily Express*, 9th July 1948; D6, *The Future is Ours,
Comrade*, Joseph Novak, The Bodley Head.

Greenhaven World History Program

History Makers
Alexander
Constantine
Leonardo Da Vinci
Columbus
Luther, Erasmus and Loyola
Napoleon
Bolivar
Adam Smith, Malthus and Marx
Darwin
Bismark
Henry Ford
Roosevelt
Stalin
Mao Tse-Tung
Gandhi
Nyerere and Nkrumah

Great Civilizations
The Ancient Near East
Ancient Greece
Pax Romana
The Middle Ages
Spices and Civilization
Chingis Khan and the Mongol Empire
Akbar and the Mughal Empire
Traditional China
Ancient America
Traditional Africa
Asoka and Indian Civilization
Mohammad and the Arab Empire
Ibin Sina and the Muslim World
Suleyman and the Ottoman Empire

Great Revolutions
The Neolithic Revolution
The Agricultural Revolution
The Scientific Revolution
The Industrial Revolution
The Communications Revolution
The American Revolution
The French Revolution
The Mexican Revolution
The Russian Revolution
The Chinese Revolution

Enduring Issues
Cities
Population
Health and Wealth
A World Economy
Law
Religion
Language
Education
The Family

Political and Social Movements
The Slave Trade
The Enlightenment
Imperialism
Nationalism
The British Raj and Indian Nationalism
The Growth of the State
The Suez Canal
The American Frontier
Japan's Modernization
Hitler's Reich
The Two World Wars
The Atom Bomb
The Cold War
The Wealth of Japan
Hollywood

DATE DUE

MAR 16 '82		
MAY 12		
OCT 28		
NOV 12		
FEB 3		
FEB 16		
MAR 27		
11/21/02		

30 505 JOSTEN'S